D0845249

SIMPLISSIME

THE SIMPLE FAMILY COOKBOOK

SIMPLISSIME

J.-F. Mallet

THE

SIMPLE

FAMILY

COOKBOOK

ilex

This book is the fruit of times spent in the kitchen with my two daughters, Jeanne and Paula. Ever since they were small children, they have been giving me ideas for easy recipes, and, for this book, they had fun inventing recipes to suit the Disney heroes and heroines who are much more familiar to them than to me. We regularly cook together as a family; it is a fun way to get them to eat everything, even spinach, broccoli, and turnips.

In addition to these wonderful shared moments, it is a way for me to make them aware of the taste of "real" food, introduce them to new ingredients, and, above all, to prepare balanced dishes for them without too much sugar and fat. As far as possible, I avoid prepacked products stuffed with hidden sugars, fats, colorings, preservatives, and other dubious substances whose impact on health is not completely known.

This does not mean that they are not occasionally allowed to treat themselves to a cheese gratin or a nice homemade hamburger. I actually try to dismiss generally accepted ideas, because a homemade burger with grilled vegetables and good-quality meat is a balanced dish. For desserts, I do not overdo the sugar or butter, but we do know how to make food we enjoy.

In this book, you will find 100 recipes, all in the style of favorite children's characters and all extremely easy to make, using a variety of easily obtainable ingredients.

I hope you share some wonderful moments, both in the kitchen and at the table.

HOW TO USE THIS BOOK

In this book, I am assuming that at home you have:

- Running water
- An oven
- A refrigerator
- A blender
- A skillet
- A Dutch oven or flameproof casserole dish
- A (sharp) knife
- A pair of scissors
- Salt and pepper
- Oil

(If this is not the case, maybe now is the time to invest!)

What are the must-have ingredients?

Fruit and vegetables: Use fresh and preferably in season, but don't hesitate to fall back on frozen raw versions. I would advise you to buy organic; after all, it is better for your children's heath, especially when you use the zest of citrus fruit and the skins of fruit and vegetables. Do not hesitate to use different varieties of vegetables.

Herbs: You can't beat fresh herbs, so try to use them when you can. If all else fails, you can always use frozen or dried versions (with the exception of oregano as it is not as good).

Oils: I prefer olive oil—always extra virgin, which is the best for your health. For the occasional variation, a drizzle of sesame oil or walnut oil can brighten up a dish and change the seasoning of a salad.

Spices: Paprika, curry powder, cumin, and turmeric feature frequently in my dishes. Spices enable you to invent new flavors, add a little touch of the exotic, and, most important, to cut down on salt. All the recipes tell you to season with salt and pepper, but I recommend using salt in moderation, because too much salt is bad for your health.

Canned goods: Stock up on cans of tuna and sardines in oil, coconut milk, and the indispensable tomato paste or diced tomatoes. That's all.

Condiments: I always have mustard, pesto, and balsamic vinegar in my pantry; they can rescue your dinner in an instant.

Which techniques should you use?

Cooking pasta: Cook in a large saucepan in plenty of boiling salted water. Pay attention to the cooking time if you like your pasta *al dente*.

Marinating: Soak an ingredient in an aromatic mixture to flavor or tenderize it.

Beating egg whites until stiff: Add a pinch of salt to the egg whites and use an electric mixer, gradually increasing the speed. Always beat the whites in the same direction to prevent them from becoming grainy.

Zesting a citrus fruit: There are two ways of zesting a citrus fruit. For beginners—and to get a fine zest—use a cheese grater on the peel of the fruit, going over each area only one time, without touching the white pith. For professionals—and to get zest that looks like vermicelli—use a zester.

Snipping with a pair of scissors: The easiest whey to prepare soft herbs, such as cilantro, is to use a pair of scissors to snip, or finely cut, them into small pieces.

What equipment should you choose?

Handheld immersion blender: Also known as a stick blender, it is used to mix liquids (soups, smoothies, milk shakes, etc.). It is a handy, inexpensive, and space-saving gadget and also means less cleaning up, because you use it directly in whatever you are mixing, with no need to transfer it to a bowl.

Blender: Used for making juices.

That's everything. All you have to do now is follow the recipe!

COCKTAIL BRIOCHE FOR THE BALL

Brioche loaf
1 large

Cream cheese
1½ cups

Cucumber
½

Tuna
1 (5-ounce) can, drained

Mint
1 bunch

 : 6

Preparation: 15 mins

• Mix the drained **tuna** with the **cream cheese**. Cut the **brioche** horizontally into six slices. Wash the **cucumber** and slice thinly. Wash the **mint** and pick off the leaves.

• Spread each slice of **brioche** with the **tuna**-and-**cream cheese** mixture, add the sliced **cucumber** and **mint** leaves, and then put the **brioche** back together.

RILLETTES IN A SARDINE CAN

Cream cheese
¾ cup

Sardines in olive oil
2 cans

Limes
2

  Salt, pepper

 : 6

Preparation: 10 mins

• Drain the **sardines** and crush them with the **cream cheese** and the zest and juice of the **limes**. Season with salt and pepper.

• Serve the rillettes in the sardine can and enjoy.

COCKTAIL BLINIS

Crème fraîche
½ cup

Chives
1 large or 2 small bunches

Smoked salmon
2 small slices

Blinis
8

 Salt, pepper

 : 4

🕐
Preparation: 10 mins

• Cut the **smoked salmon** into thin strips.

• Snip the **chives** with scissors, saving a few for decoration, and mix with the **crème fraîche**. Season with salt and pepper.

• When it is time to serve, spread the **crème fraîche** mixture on the **blinis**, top with the **salmon** strips, and enjoy.

JUDY HOPPS'S CARROTS WITH ORANGE

Small carrots
1 bunch

Greek-style yogurt
1 cup

Orange
1

Cilantro
1 bunch, chopped

  **Salt, pepper**

🍴 : 4

🕐
Preparation: 5 mins

• Trim and wash the **carrots**. Cut the largest ones in half.

• Mix the **yogurt** with the zest and juice of the **orange** and the **cilantro**. Season with salt and pepper.

• Eat the **carrots** with the dip.

MULAN'S CRISPY CRACKERS

Taramosalata ½ (7-ounce) container	**Shrimp crackers** 12

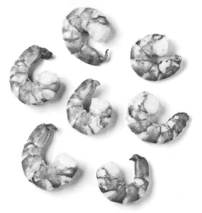

Shrimp 6, cooked and peeled	**Mint** 12 leaves

 : 4

Preparation: 5 mins

• Just before serving (so the crackers do not become soggy), place a little **taramosalata**, 1 **mint** leaf, and ½ **shrimp** on each **cracker**.

BEAUTY'S BOUQUET OF ROSES

Cape gooseberries
12

Coppa or other ham
12 thin slices

 : 4

Preparation: 5 mins

• Carefully peel back the **Cape gooseberry leaves**.

• Wrap each **berry** in one slice of **ham**.

• Arrange on a dish and enjoy.

PONGO'S NIBBLES

Pizza dough
1 rectangular

Ground beef
7 ounces, lean

Mustard
2 tablespoons

Grated Parmesan
¼ cup

 **Salt, pepper**

🐭 : 4

⏱

Preparation: 10 mins
Refrigeration: 30 mins
Cooking time: 15 mins

- Preheat the oven to 400°F.
- Mix together the **ground beef**, **mustard**, and half the **Parmesan**. Season with salt and pepper.
- Spread the meat over the **pizza dough**. Roll the sides toward the center and chill in the fridge.
- Cut the roll into slices. Arrange on a baking sheet lined with parchment paper. Sprinkle with the remaining **Parmesan** and bake for 15 mins.

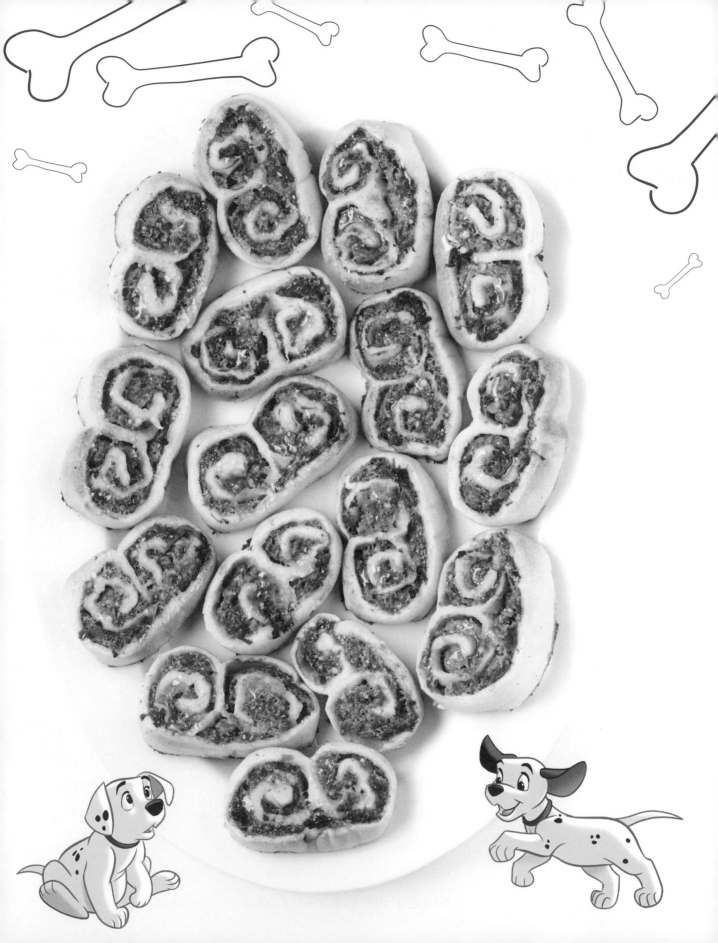

HUMMUS WITH CUMIN

Chickpeas 3⅓ cups canned	**Olive oil** 6 tablespoons

Garlic 2 cloves	**Lemons** 2	**Cumin seeds** 1 teaspoon

 Salt, pepper

 : 4

⏱

Preparation: 10 mins

• Drain and rinse the **chickpeas** (garbanzo beans). Heat in a saucepan with ¼ cup water.

• Mix the **chickpeas** with the cooking water, 5 tablespoons of the **olive oil**, the chopped **garlic**, the juice of the **lemons**, and half the **cumin**. Season with salt and pepper and let cool.

• Transfer to a serving dish and drizzle with the remaining **oil** and **cumin seeds**.

MULAN'S SPRING ROLLS

Spring roll wrappers 8 large	**Cucumber** ½

Cooked ham 4 slices	**Mint** 2 bunches	**Shrimp** 16, cooked and peeled

: 4

Preparation: 15 mins

• Moisten the **wrappers** under cold running water. Top with the **shrimp** cut in half, slices of **ham** cut in half, **cucumber** cut in sticks, and **mint** leaves.

• Turn in the edges, roll up tightly, and enjoy.

ABUELITA'S GUACAMOLE

Avocados
2

Smoked salmon
4 small slices

Limes
2

Ground cumin
1 teaspoon

Cilantro
1 bunch

 Salt, pepper

🐭 : 4

⏱ Preparation: 5 mins

• Peel the **avocados**, remove the pits, and mix the flesh with the juice of the **limes** and the **cumin**. Season with salt and pepper.
• Arrange the **guacamole** on a dish and add the **smoked salmon** cut into pieces.
• Sprinkle with **cilantro** leaves and enjoy.

HAWAIIAN SALAD

Pineapple
1 small

Rice
½ cup

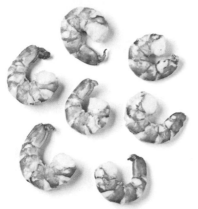

Shrimp
3½ ounces, cooked and peeled

Olive oil
2 tablespoons

Cooked ham
2 slices

 Salt, pepper

: 4

Preparation: 10 mins
Cooking time: 10 mins

• Cook the **rice** in boiling salted water and let cool.

• Cut the **pineapple** in half lengthwise, scoop out the flesh, and cut into small pieces. Chop the **ham** and mix it with the **pineapple**, **rice**, **shrimp**, and **olive oil**. Season with salt and pepper.

• Arrange the salad in the **pineapple shells** and enjoy.

TROPICAL-STYLE FISH

Salmon steaks
4, skinless

Coconut milk
1 cup

Limes
4

Cilantro
2 bunches

Cucumber
¼

Salt, pepper

: 4

Preparation: 5 mins
Refrigeration: 30 mins

• Cut the **salmon steaks** into cubes and mix with the juice of the **limes**, sliced **cucumber**, **coconut milk**, and **cilantro**, snipped with scissors.

• Season with salt and pepper. Marinate for 30 mins in the refrigerator and serve.

MICKEY AND FRIENDS' SALAD

Corn kernels
1¼ cups, canned

Roma tomatoes
4

Paprika
2 tablespoons

Avocado
1

Lemons
2

  Salt, pepper

 Olive oil

 **: 4**

🕐

Preparation: 10 mins

- Cut the **tomatoes** in half lengthwise and seed.
- Cut the **avocado** into small cubes, mix with the **corn kernels**, and spoon into the **tomatoes**.
- Mix the **paprika** with the juice of the **lemons** and 3 tablespoons of olive oil. Season with salt and pepper, pour over the **tomatoes**, and serve.

SUMMER RATATOUILLE

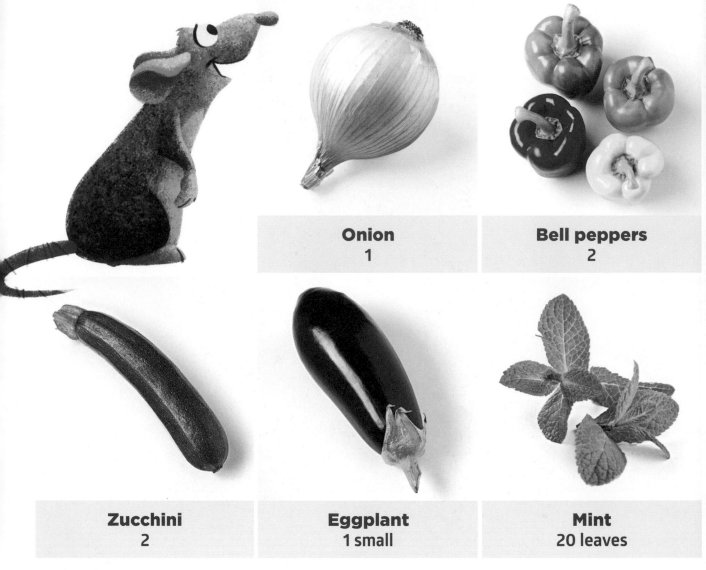

Onion 1	Bell peppers 2
Zucchini 2	Eggplant 1 small	Mint 20 leaves

 Salt, pepper

 Olive oil

 : 4

Preparation: 25 mins
Cooking time: 45 mins

• Cut the **onion**, **bell peppers**, **zucchini**, and **eggplant** into small pieces.

• Heat 6 tablespoons of olive oil and sauté the vegetables without browning. Season with salt and pepper and simmer for 45 mins over low heat.

• Let cool, add the **mint**, snipped with scissors, and serve.

THE EMPEROR'S CEVICHE

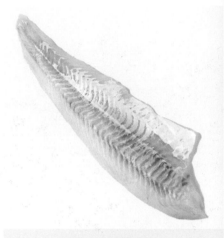

Cucumber
1

Cod fillets
2

Limes
4

Coconut milk
1 cup

Cilantro
2 tablespoons

 **Salt, pepper**

 Olive oil

❍ : 4

⊘
Preparation: 5 mins
Marination: 10 mins

• Cut the **cucumber** in half lengthwise and scoop out the flesh. Cut into eight boats.

• Cut the **cod** into pieces and mix with the **cucumber** flesh, **coconut milk**, juice of the **limes**, 2 tablespoons of olive oil, and **cilantro**, snipped with scissors. Marinate for 10 mins and arrange in the **cucumber** boats. Season with salt and pepper and serve.

36

NANI'S SALAD

Romaine lettuce
2

Mixed seafood
10 ounces, frozen

Blueberries
1 cup

Olive oil
6 tablespoons

Soy sauce
¼ cup

  Pepper

🐭 : 4

🕐

Preparation: 10 mins
Cooking time: 5 mins

• Cut the **lettuce** in half lengthwise, then remove and chop up the hearts a little.

• Sauté the **seafood** for 5 mins in a saucepan with the **olive oil** and **soy sauce**. Let cool, then mix with the **blueberries** and chopped **lettuce**.

• Arrange in the **lettuce**, pour over the cooking juices, season with pepper, and serve.

PACHA'S SALAD

Red quinoa ⅔ cup	**Passion fruits** 4

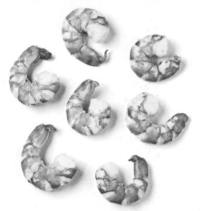

Shrimp 16, cooked and peeled	**Cilantro** 1 bunch

🧂 **Salt, pepper**

🫗 **Olive oil**

 : 4

⏱

Preparation: 5 mins
Cooking time: 10 mins
Resting time: 10 mins

• Cook the **quinoa** for 10 mins in 1 cup of water with the lid on. Turn off the heat and let swell for 10 mins.

• Cut the **passion fruits** in half. Scoop out the flesh and mix with the cold **quinoa**, snipped **cilantro**, and the chopped **shrimp**. Season.

• Fill the **passion fruit** shells with the mixture and drizzle with olive oil.

DUCHESS'S LIGHT SUPPER

Tuna in brine
2 (5-ounce) cans

Arugula
5 cups

Eggs
5

  **Salt, pepper**

  Butter
(for greasing)

 : 4

🕐
Preparation: 5 mins
Cooking time: 30 mins

• Preheat the oven to 350°F.
• Drain the **tuna**, mix with the beaten **eggs** and 3½ cups of the **arugula**, snipped with scissors, and season with salt and pepper.
• Transfer to a greased loaf pan and bake for 30 mins.
• Serve cold in thick slices with the remainder of the **arugula**.

DUMBO'S FAVORITE SALAD

Unshelled peanuts
1 cup

Shredded carrots
2 cups

Cilantro
2 bunches

Soy sauce
3 tablespoons

Lemongrass
2 stalks

 **Salt, pepper**

Peanut oil

 : 4

Preparation: 10 mins

• Shell the **peanuts**. Slice the **lemongrass**. Wash the **cilantro** and snip coarsely with scissors.

• When you are about to eat, mix all of the ingredients together in a salad bowl with 2 tablespoons of peanut oil, season with salt and pepper, and serve.

44

FALL SALAD

Oak leaf lettuce
1

Walnuts
25 halves

Black grapes
2 bunches

Walnut oil
2 tablespoons

Balsamic vinegar
2 tablespoons

 **Salt, pepper**

:4

Preparation: 5 mins

• Wash the **grapes** and cut in half. Coarsely crush the **walnut** halves. Wash the **lettuce** and pick off the leaves.

• When you are about to eat, mix all the ingredients together in a salad bowl, season with salt and pepper, and serve.

CORN PANCAKES

Romaine lettuce
1

Corn kernels
2 cups, canned

All-purpose flour
2 tablespoons

Eggs
2

Grated Parmesan
¼ cup

 Salt, pepper

 Oil

 **: 4**

Preparation: 15 mins
Cooking time: 10 mins

• Blend the **corn kernels** with the **eggs** and **flour**. Season with salt and pepper. Heat 3 tablespoons of oil in a large skillet and add tablespoons of batter to form small pancakes. Cook for 1 min on each side.

• Chop the **lettuce** and mix with 1 tablespoon of oil and the **Parmesan**. Season with salt and pepper, add the warm pancakes, and serve.

48

MINNIE'S GREEN SALAD

Green beans
2 cups

Zucchini
2

Peas
1⅓ cups, fresh or frozen

Boston lettuce
2

 Salt, pepper

Olive oil

 : 4

Mint
20 leaves

Preparation: 15 mins
Cooking time: 10 mins

• Cook the **green beans**, sliced **zucchini**, and **peas** for 10 mins in boiling salted water. Drain and rinse in cold water.

• Separate the **lettuce** leaves and mix with the vegetables and **mint**.

• Season with salt and pepper and a drizzle of olive oil and serve.

MUSHU'S SALAD

Chicken breasts
2

Sesame oil
¼ cup

Sesame seeds
¼ cup

Cilantro
1 bunch

Bean sprouts
2 cups

 Salt, pepper

 : 4

Preparation: 5 mins
Cooking time: 5 mins

- Coarsely snip the **cilantro** with scissors and arrange on a dish with the **bean sprouts**.
- Chop the **chicken breasts** and sauté over high heat with the **oil** and **sesame seeds**. Season with salt and pepper.
- Arrange on the dish with the cooking juices and serve immediately.

MOUNT OLYMPUS TOMATOES

Mint
1 bunch

Greek yogurt
⅔ cup

Garlic
2 cloves

Tomatoes
4

Cucumber
½

  Salt, pepper

 **Olive oil**

: 4

Preparation: 10 mins

• Snip the **mint**, setting a few leaves aside. Peel the **garlic**. Grate the **cucumber** and **garlic** and mix with the **mint** and **yogurt**.

• Cut the **tomatoes** in half, seed, and top with the sauce. Season with salt and pepper.

• Add the remaining **mint** leaves and serve with a drizzle of olive oil.

MR. SMEE'S SOUP

Watermelon
½ small

Zucchini
2

Mint
1 bunch

  Salt, pepper

Olive oil

 : 4

🕐

Preparation: 10 mins
Cooking time: 20 mins

• Chop up the **zucchini** and cook over low heat in 1¾ cups water for 20 mins. Let cool. Blend the soup with three-quarters of the **mint**, using an immersion blender. Season with salt and pepper.
• Scoop the flesh out of the **watermelon** and chop. Pour the soup into the **melon** shell and add the flesh and remaining **mint**. Serve with a drizzle of olive oil.

VITAMIN-RICH GAZPACHO

Tomatoes 4	Cucumber ½
Basil 1 bunch	Kiwis 2

 Salt, pepper

🐭 : 4

⏱
Preparation: 5 mins

• Cut the **cucumber**, **tomatoes**, and **kiwis** into small pieces, but set aside four slices of **kiwi**.

• Put everything into a blender, add the **basil**, and 1 cup of water. Season with salt and pepper and blend.

• Spoon into bowls. Place one slice of **kiwi** on each bowl and serve.

RÉMY'S FAMOUS SOUP

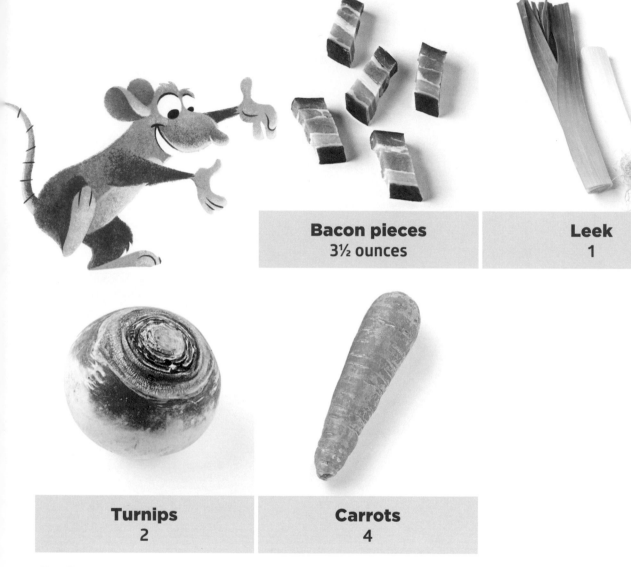

Bacon pieces	Leek
3½ ounces	1

Turnips	Carrots
2	4

Salt, pepper

: 4

Preparation: 5 mins
Cooking time: 35 mins

• Peel the **leek**, **turnips** and **carrots**, chop into small pieces and place in a saucepan with the **bacon** and 4 cups of water, and cover with a lid.

• Bring to the boil, then simmer for 30 mins over low heat. Add a little more water if too much has evaporated.

• Season with salt and pepper and serve.

SOUP OF THE FOREST

Cranberries
2 tablespoons

Oyster mushrooms
7 ounces

Blueberries
1 cup

Chanterelles
7 ounces

Bacon pieces
7 ounces

 Salt, pepper

🐭 : 4

🕐
Preparation: 10 mins
Cooking time: 20 mins

• Wash the **mushrooms** and remove the stems.
• Sauté the **bacon pieces** for 1 min over high heat in a dry saucepan. Add all the **mushrooms** and brown for 5 mins, stirring continuously. Add the **blueberries**, **cranberries**, and 3 cups of water.
• Season with salt and pepper and simmer for 15 mins over low heat before serving.

FAIRY GODMOTHER'S MAGIC SOUP

Pumpkin
1, about 3½ pounds

Whole-grain bread
4 large slices

Cheddar cheese
1½ cups shredded

🧂🧂 **Salt, pepper**

🐭 : 4–6

⏱

Preparation: 20 mins
Cooking time: 45 mins

• Preheat the oven to 350°F.
• Cut a lid off the **pumpkin**. Scoop out the flesh and cut into pieces. Cook for 15 mins, just covered with water, then blend. Cut the slices of **bread** in half. Fill the **pumpkin** with alternate layers of soup, **bread**, and **cheese**, seasoning each layer with salt and pepper. Bake in the oven for 30 mins and serve.

THE FLASH BURGER

Hamburger buns
4, cut in half

Zucchini
3

Ground beef
14 ounces, lean

Eggplants
2

Tomatoes
6

 Salt, pepper

Oil

 : 4

Preparation: 15 mins
Cooking time: 50 mins

• Preheat the oven to 400°F.
• Slice the **vegetables** thinly and bake for 35 mins on a baking sheet with 2 tablespoons of oil. Season with salt and pepper.
• Meanwhile, shape the **ground beef** into four patties, season them, and fry in one tablespoon of oil over medium heat until cooked through, turning once. Assemble and serve hot.

JOHN SMITH'S CORN ON THE COB

Ears of corn
4, shucked

Paprika
1 tablespoon

Curry powder
1 tablespoon

Dried oregano
1 tablespoon

Feta
½ cup, crumbled

 Salt, pepper

🐭 : 4

🕐
Preparation: 5 mins
Cooking time: 15 mins

• Cook the **ears of corn** for 15 mins in boiling water or steam.

• Sprinkle the corn with the **curry powder**, **paprika**, and **oregano** while still hot.

• Sprinkle with the **feta**. Season with salt and pepper and serve.

TURKEY NUGGETS

Turkey scallops
4

Eggs
2

Cornflakes
5 cups

Greek-style yogurt
1 cup

Curry powder
3 tablespoons

 Salt, pepper

 **: 4**

Preparation: 15 mins
Cooking time: 15 mins

- Preheat the oven to 350°F.
- Crush the **cornflakes**. Beat the **eggs**.
- Cut the **turkey** into strips, then dip them into the **egg** and then the **cornflakes**. Arrange on a baking sheet lined with parchment paper, season with salt and pepper and bake for 15 mins.
- Mix the **yogurt** with the **curry powder** and serve with the nuggets.

SWEET POTATO OVEN FRIES

Sweet potatoes
2

Red bell pepper
1

Tomatoes
3

Honey
2 tablespoons

Paprika
2 tablespoons

  Salt, pepper

 **Oil**

: 4

Preparation: 10 mins
Cooking time: 40 mins

72

• Preheat the oven to 350°F.

• Peel the **sweet potatoes** and cut into sticks. Arrange on a baking sheet with 2 tablespoons of oil. Season and bake for 20 mins.

• Chop up the **bell pepper** and **tomatoes**. Sauté in a saucepan with the **honey** and **paprika**, reduce the heat, and cook for 20 mins. Season, blend, and serve with the fries.

POTATO WEDGES WITH CHIVE SAUCE

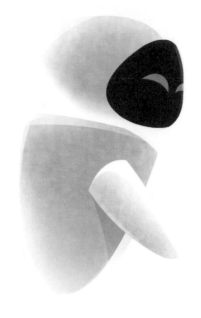

Chives
1 bunch

New red potatoes
1¾ pounds

Paprika
2 tablespoons

Oil
2 tablespoons

Greek-style yogurt
1¼ cups

 Salt, pepper

 **: 4**

Preparation: 5 mins
Cooking time: 45 mins

- Preheat the oven to 350°F.
- Wash the **potatoes**, cut into wedges, and mix in a large bowl with the **oil** and **paprika**. Season with salt and pepper.
- Bake for 45 mins on a baking sheet lined with parchment paper.
- Beat the **yogurt** with the chopped **chives** and serve with the **potato wedges**.

MIGUEL'S FAVORITE EMPANADA

Empanada (pastry) dough
1

Ground beef
9 ounces, lean

Mozzarella
2 balls, chopped

Ground cumin
2 tablespoons

 Salt, pepper

 **: 2**

Preparation: 10 mins
Cooking time: 30 mins

• Preheat the oven to 400°F.
• Unroll the **empanada dough** on its parchment paper on a baking sheet. Brown the **ground beef** then mix with the **cumin** and the **mozzarella** and season.
• Spread the mixture over half the **dough**. Fold it over and press the edges together with a fork. Bake for 25 mins.

PIZZA PLANET SPECIAL

Pizza dough
1

Ground beef
10½ ounces, lean

Tomato sauce
¼ cup

Dried oregano
2 tablespoons

Mozzarella
1 ball

Salt, pepper

Oil

: 4

**Preparation: 5 mins
Cooking time: approx
20 mins**

- Preheat the oven to 400°F.
- Cut the **mozzarella** into big chunks. Form the **meat** into eight balls and brown in a pan with oil. Place the **pizza dough** on a baking sheet. Spread the **tomato sauce** over the entire surface of the **pizza dough**. Add the **mozzarella** and the meatballs. Sprinkle with **oregano** and season.
- Bake until the dough is crisp and serve.

78

HAWAIIAN PIZZA

Pizza dough
1

Tomato sauce
¼ cup

Pineapple in syrup
4 slices

Cooked ham
2 slices

Grated Parmesan
2 tablespoons

  Salt, pepper

 : 4

🕐
Preparation: 5 mins
Cooking time: 25 mins

• Place the **pizza dough** on a baking sheet lined with parchment paper. Spread the **tomato sauce** over the entire **pizza dough**.

• Add the **ham** cut into pieces and the slices of **pineapple**. Sprinkle with the **Parmesan**. Season with salt and pepper.

• Bake in the oven for 25 mins and serve.

VEGGIE PIZZA WITH CHEESE

Pizza dough
1 rectangular

Tomatoes
3

Zucchini
1 large

Green bell pepper
1

Cheddar cheese
1 cup shredded

 Salt, pepper

 : 4–6

⏱
Preparation: 10 mins
Cooking time: 35 mins

• Preheat the oven to 400°F.
• Place the **pizza dough** on a baking sheet lined with parchment paper.
• Slice the **vegetables** thinly, distribute them over the **crust**, and season with salt and pepper. Sprinkle with the **cheese** and bake in the oven for 35 mins.
• Serve hot or cold.

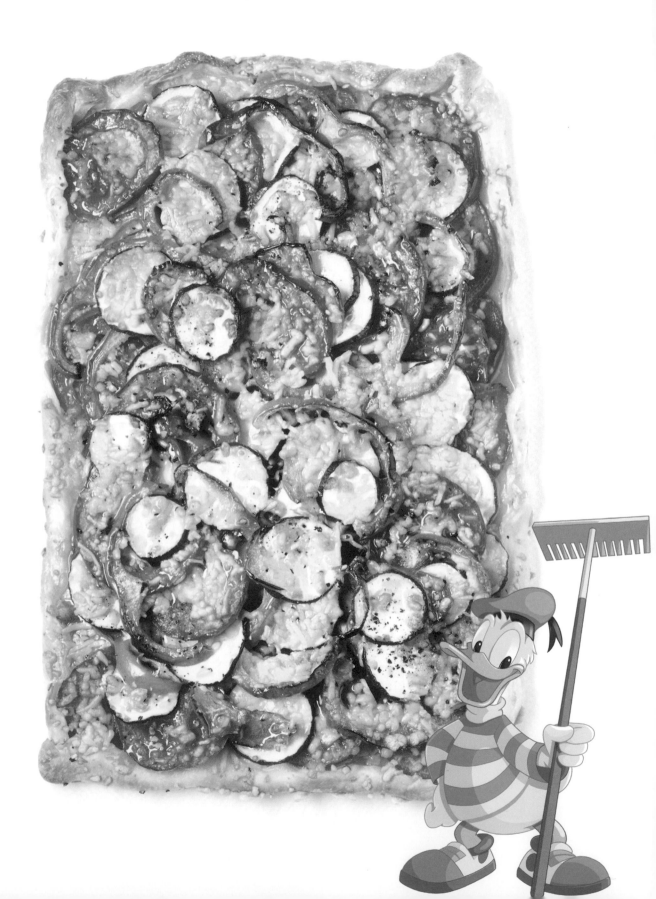

GEPPETTO'S TORTELLINI

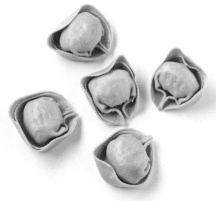

Tortellini
9 ounces, spinach and ricotta

Coppa or other ham
4 thin slices

Basil
1 bunch

Pine nuts
⅓ cup

 Salt, pepper

 Olive oil

 : 4

Preparation: 5 mins
Cooking time: 10 mins

• Cook the **tortellini** according to the package directions in boiling water, then drain.

• Brown the **pine nuts** in a skillet for 30 seconds, add the **tortellini** and **ham**, and cook for 1 min, stirring continuously.

• Turn off the heat, add the **basil**, and season with salt and pepper. Mix, and serve with a drizzle of olive oil.

TONY'S SPAGHETTI

Spaghetti
10½ ounces

Sausage meat
14 ounces

Tomato passata
2 cups

Bouquets garnis
2, bay leaves and thyme

Onion
1 large

🧂 Salt, pepper

🫗 Oil

🐭 : 4

⏱
Preparation: 10 mins
Cooking time: 40 mins

• Form the **meat** into 12 balls. Chop the **onion**.
• Sauté the **meatballs** and **onion** in a skillet with 1 tablespoon of oil over high heat for 5 mins. Add the **tomato passata** and **bouquets garnis** and season. Reduce the heat to low and simmer for 25 mins.
• Serve with the **spaghetti** cooked according to the package directions.

AUNT CASS'S SOBA

Buckwheat noodles 150 g	**Peas** 1⅓ cups, fresh or frozen

Sesame oil ¼ cup	**Sesame seeds** ⅓ cup	**Eggs** 4

 Salt, pepper

 : 4

Preparation: 10 mins
Cooking time: 10 mins

- Boil the **eggs** for exactly 5 mins, drain, cool, and then peel carefully.
- Plunge the **noodles** and **peas** into boiling salted water for 5 mins. Drain and mix with the **sesame seeds** and **oil**. Season with salt and pepper.
- Serve with the halved **eggs**.

THE ARISTOCATS' SPAGHETTI

Spaghetti
10½ ounces

Sardines in oil
2 cans

Rusk toasts or flatbread
4

Arugula
3 cups

Dried garlic
1 teaspoon

 Salt, pepper

🐭 : 4

🕐
Preparation: 5 mins
Cooking time: 10 mins

• Cook the **spaghetti** in boiling salted water according to the package directions. Drain and transfer to a skillet with 1 tablespoon of cooking water, the **sardines** cut into pieces with the oil from 1 can, coarsely crumbled **toasts**, and **dried garlic**. Cook for 2 mins, stirring continuously.
• Remove from the heat, add the **arugula** and mix. Season with pepper, and serve immediately.

LADY'S PASTA

Spaghetti 10½ ounces	**Ground beef** 14 ounces, lean

Basil 20 leaves	**Cherry tomatoes** 16	**Onion** 1 (thinly sliced)

 Salt, pepper

 Olive oil

 Grated Parmesan

 : 4

Preparation: 10 mins
Cooking time: 45 mins

• Heat some oil in a Dutch oven or casserole dish and lightly brown the **onion** and **ground beef**.
• Add the **tomatoes** cut in half and 2 cups of water and cook over low heat for 30 mins.
• Cook the **spaghetti** in boiling salted water according to the package directions and drain.
• Add the **spaghetti** and **basil** to the sauce, cook for 5 mins, then serve with **Parmesan**.

OMELET FOR LINGUINI

Eggs 8	**Butter** 4 teaspoons

Swiss or cheddar cheese 1 cup shredded	**Basil** 2 bunches

  Salt, pepper

Oil

 : 4

Preparation: 5 mins
Cooking time: 5 mins

• Beat the **eggs** with a fork, add the **basil** leaves snipped with scissors, and the **shredded cheese**. Season with salt and pepper.

• Melt the **butter** in a skillet with 1 tablespoon of oil and pour in the omelet mixture

• Cook for 4–5 mins, stirring regularly, until the **eggs** are completely cooked. Transfer the omelet to a dish and serve immediately.

STUFFED MUSHROOMS

Mushrooms
8 large

Dried oregano
1 tablespoon

Cream cheese
⅔ cup

 Salt, pepper

 Olive oil

: 4

Preparation: 15 mins
Cooking time: 25 mins

• Preheat the oven to 350°F.
• Wash the **mushrooms**. Cut off and chop the stems, then mix them with the **cream cheese** and **oregano**. Season with salt and pepper. Stuff the **mushrooms** with the mixture.
• Place the **mushrooms** in an ovenproof dish and bake for 25 mins. Serve with a drizzle of olive oil.

EGGPLANTS STUFFED WITH RATATOUILLE

Eggplants 2	Herbes de Provence 1 tablespoon

Cheddar cheese 1 cup, shredded	Tomatoes 4	Zucchini 1

  Salt, pepper

: 4

Preparation: 15 mins
Cooking time: 45 mins

- Preheat the oven to 400°F.
- Cut the **eggplants** in half and scoop out the flesh
- Dice the **eggplant** flesh, **tomatoes**, and **zucchini**. Mix with the **herbes de Provence**, season with salt and pepper, and spoon into the **eggplant** shells.
- Place in an ovenproof dish with 3 cups of water.
- Sprinkle with the **cheese** and bake for 45 mins.

HIRO'S FAVORITE YAKITORIS

Chicken breasts
3

Sesame seeds
2 tablespoons

Shiitake mushrooms
10

Soy sauce
½ cup

 Salt, pepper

 : 4

⏱
Preparation: 10 mins
Cooking time: 10 mins
Marination: 20 mins

• Preheat the oven to 350°F.
• Cut the **mushrooms** and **chicken** into small pieces. Assemble 12 skewers with alternate pieces of **chicken** and **mushroom**. Place in an ovenproof dish. Add the **sesame seeds** and **soy sauce** and marinate for 20 mins.
• Bake in the oven for 10 mins and serve with the cooking juices.

HECTOR'S CHORIZO SAUTÉ

Baby corn
24

Whole chorizo sausage
½

Cherry tomatoes
20

Cilantro
1 bunch

  Salt, pepper

🐭 **: 4**

🕐
Preparation: 6 mins
Cooking time: 6 mins

• Sauté the **baby corn** and sliced **chorizo** over high heat for 5 mins.

• Add the **cherry tomatoes**. Season with salt and pepper and cook for another min.

• Serve immediately with the **cilantro** leaves.

GUSTEAU'S RATATOUILLE

Basil
1 bunch

Tomatoes
6

Zucchini
4

Cooked ham
4 slices

Eggplant
1

 Salt, pepper

: 4–5

Preparation: 15 mins
Cooking time: 30 mins

- Preheat the oven to 400°F.
- Wash all the **vegetables** and slice them thinly without peeling. Arrange in a large ovenproof dish, interspersed with slices of **ham** cut into quarters and the **basil** leaves.
- Season with salt and pepper. Bake for 30 mins and serve.

HEROES' SKEWERS

Chicken legs
4

New red potatoes
4

Limes
2

Red onions
2

Thyme
4 sprigs, fresh or dried

 Salt, pepper

 Oil

 **: 4**

🕐
Preparation: 10 mins
Cooking time: 45 mins

• Preheat the oven to 350°F.

• Cut one **lime** into eight slices, the **potatoes** in half and the **onions** into quarters.

• Assemble four skewers, using all the ingredients in turn. Place the skewers in an ovenproof dish and add 2 tablespoons of oil, the juice of the remaining **lime**, and the **thyme**. Season with salt and pepper and bake for 45 mins.

SKINNER'S PEAS

Peas
2⅔ cups, fresh or frozen

Onion
1

Boston lettuce
2

Smoked sausages
2

  **Salt, pepper**

 Oil

 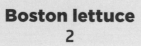 **: 4**

🕐

Preparation: 10 mins
Cooking time: 20 mins

• In a Dutch oven or casserole dish with 2 tablespoons of oil, sauté the chopped **onion** and sliced **sausages** for 5 mins. Add the sliced **lettuce** and the **peas**. Cook for 15 mins, stirring occasionally.

• Season with salt and pepper and serve.

PINOCCHIO'S SALTIMBOCCA

Veal scallops
4 small, flattened

Baby spinach
2 cups

Mozzarella
1 ball

Prosciutto ham
4 thin slices

Rosemary
4 sprigs

 Salt, pepper

 **: 4**

Preparation: 5 mins
Cooking time: 20 mins

- Preheat the oven to 350°F.
- Place the slices of **ham** on the **veal scallops**. Top with the **baby spinach** and **mozzarella** cut into pieces.
- Roll up and fasten with a sprig of **rosemary**. Place in an ovenproof dish, season with salt and pepper, and bake for 20 mins.

PORK WITH PINEAPPLE

Pork chops
4

Pineapple in syrup
2 slices

Soy sauce
½ cup

Cilantro
1 bunch

 Oil

 : 4

🕐
Preparation: 5 mins
Cooking time: 25 mins

• Fry the **pork chops** for 2 mins in a saucepan with 1 tablespoon of oil. Add the chopped **pineapple**, ⅓ cup of its syrup, and the **soy sauce**, reduce the heat, and cook for 20 mins, basting occasionally with the cooking juices.

• Add the **cilantro**, snipped with scissors, and serve.

AGRABAH LAMB WITH POMEGRANATE

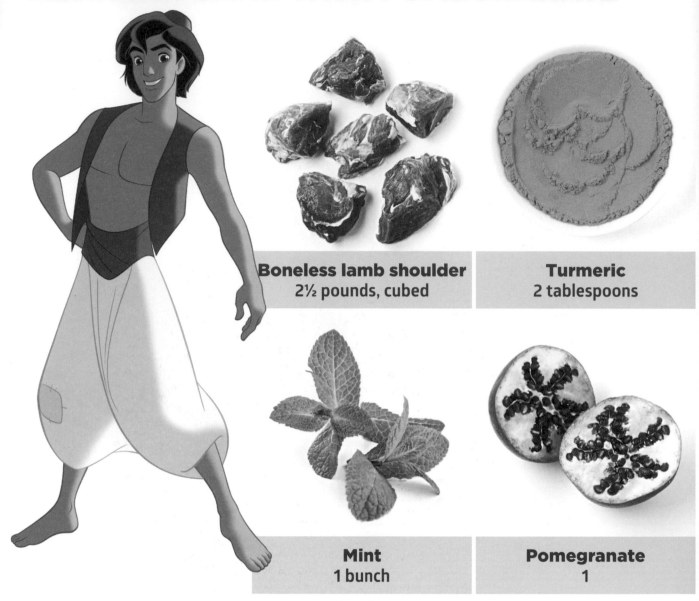

Boneless lamb shoulder
2½ pounds, cubed

Turmeric
2 tablespoons

Mint
1 bunch

Pomegranate
1

 Salt, pepper

 Oil

 : 4

⏱
Preparation: 5 mins
Cooking time: 1 hour 30 mins

• In a Dutch oven or casserole dish, cook the pieces of **lamb** in 2 tablespoons of oil.

• Add the **turmeric** and 2 cups of water. Season with salt and pepper and mix. Reduce the heat, cover, and simmer over low heat for 1 hour 30 mins.

• Scoop the seeds out of the **pomegranate**, add to the **lamb**, and serve with the **mint**.

FAIRIES' CASSEROLE

Lamb shanks
4, without fat

Bouquets garnis
2, bay leaves and thyme

Peas
4 cups, fresh or frozen

Mint
1 bunch

 **Salt, pepper**

🐭 : 4

🕐
Preparation: 5 mins
Cooking time: 2 hours

• Preheat the oven to 400°F.
• Place the **lamb shanks** in a Dutch oven or casserole dish with the **bouquets garnis** and 2 cups of water, season with salt and pepper, cover, and cook in the oven for 1 hour 30 mins.
• Add the **peas** and **mint** snipped with scissors. Cook for another 30 mins and serve.

GRANDMOTHER FA'S CHINESE-STYLE PORK

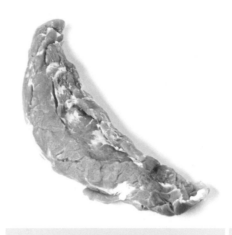

Pork tenderloin
14 ounces

Red bell peppers
2

Ginger
2-inch piece

Soy sauce
½ cup

Roasted cashew nuts
1 cup

 Oil

: 4

Preparation: 5 mins
Cooking time: 20 mins

• Cut the **pork tenderloin** into pieces and peel the **bell peppers** and **ginger**.
• Fry the **meat**, **ginger**, and **bell peppers** lightly in a saucepan with 1 tablespoon of oil.
• Add the **soy sauce** and **cashew nuts**, then cook for 15 mins over low heat, stirring occasionally.

ROOT VEGETABLE STEW

Bouquets garnis
2, bay leaves and thyme

Rib of beef
2½ pounds

Yellow carrots
3

Parsnips
2

Golden Ball turnips
3

  Salt, pepper

🐭 : 4

🕐
**Preparation: 10 mins
Cooking time: 2 hours
45 mins**

• Put the **beef** into a Dutch oven or casserole dish, add 5 cups of water, cover, and simmer over low heat for 2 hours.

• Peel the **vegetables** and add them to the dish with the **bouquets garnis**. Season with salt and pepper, cook for another 45 mins, and serve.

CINDERELLA'S STUFFED SQUASH

Red kuri squash
2

Chicken breasts
2

Shredded carrot
1⅓ cups

Grated Parmesan
¼ cup

 Salt, pepper

 **: 4**

🕐

Preparation: 10 mins
Cooking time: 40 mins

- Preheat the oven to 350°F.
- Cut the **chicken** into pieces and mix with the **shredded carrot** and the **Parmesan**. Season with salt and pepper.
- Cut each **squash** in half, scoop out the contents, and stuff with the **chicken** mixture.
- Bake in an ovenproof dish for 40 mins and serve hot.

THE SNUGGLY DUCKLING'S CASSEROLE

Boneless beef chuck
2½ pounds, cubed

Fava beans
1⅓ cup, shelled and frozen

Carrots with greens
1 bunch

Bouquets garnis
3, bay leaves and thyme

 Salt, pepper

 **Oil**

 : 4

⏱
**Preparation: 5 mins
Cooking time: 2 hours
40 mins**

• In a Dutch oven, lightly brown the **beef** with 3 tablespoons of oil for 10 mins. Season with salt and pepper. Add 8½ cups of water and the **bouquets garnis**. Cover and simmer over low heat for 2 hours.

• Add the peeled **carrots** (cut into pieces if large) and the **beans**. Cook over low heat for 30 mins with the lid on.

MOUSSAKA

Eggplants 2	**Ground beef** 14 ounces, lean

Tomato passata 2 cups	**Dried oregano** 2 tablespoons	**Feta cheese** ⅓ cup crumbled

 Salt, pepper

 Olive oil

 **: 4**

⏱

Preparation: 5 mins
Cooking time: 45 mins

- Preheat the oven to 350°F.
- Cut the **eggplants** into pieces and mix in an ovenproof dish with the **ground beef**, **tomato passata**, and **oregano**. Season with salt and pepper and sprinkle with the **feta cheese**.
- Bake in the oven for 45 mins and serve with a drizzle of olive oil.

PONGO'S MEATBALLS

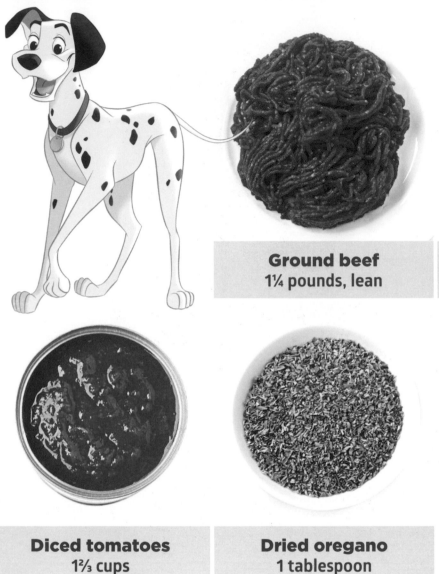

Ground beef
1¼ pounds, lean

Cheddar cheese
¾ cup shredded

Diced tomatoes
1⅔ cups

Dried oregano
1 tablespoon

Salt, pepper

Olive oil

: 4

Preparation: 5 mins
Cooking time: approx
25 mins

• Preheat the oven to 400°F.
• Mix the **ground beef** with the **cheese** and **oregano**. Form eight meatballs and season with salt and pepper. Arrange in an ovenproof dish with the **diced tomatoes**.
• Bake until the meatballs are cooked through and serve with a drizzle of olive oil.

THE INCREDIBLES' SUPER STEAK

Steaks	Broccoli
4	1 large head

Olive oil	Garlic
2 tablespoons	4 cloves

  Salt, pepper

:4

Preparation: 10 mins
Cooking time: 11 mins

• Cut the **steaks** into pieces and leave until room temperature. Peel and slice the **garlic**. Cut up the **broccoli** and blanch for 5 mins in boiling water.

• Sauté the **garlic** for 1 min in a saucepan with the **olive oil**. Add the pieces of **steak** and cook to your liking.

• Add the **broccoli** and cook for 3 mins, stirring continuously. Season and serve immediately.

FLYNN'S QUAILS WITH MUSHROOMS

Quails
4

Wild mushrooms
1¼ pounds, only caps

Chicken broth
1¼ cups

Bouquets garnis
2, bay leaves and thyme

 Salt, pepper

 **Oil**

: 4

Preparation: 10 mins
Cooking time: 45 mins

- Brown the **quails** lightly in a Dutch oven or casserole dish with 2 tablespoons of oil for 10 mins, stirring continuously.
- Pour in the **broth** and add the washed **mushrooms** caps and the **bouquets garnis**.
- Season with salt and pepper, reduce the heat to low, cover, simmer for 35 mins, and serve.

TIANA'S JAMBALAYA

Chicken legs
4

Smoked sausages
2

Paprika
2 tablespoons

Rice
2 cups

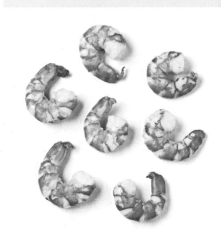

Shrimp
7 ounces, cooked and peeled

 **Salt, pepper**

🐭 : 4

🕐

Preparation: 5 mins
Cooking time: 45 mins

- Preheat the oven to 400°F.
- In an ovenproof dish, mix together the **rice**, **chicken legs**, **shrimp**, **smoked sausages** cut into pieces, 4 cups of water, and the **paprika**. Season with salt and pepper and mix again.
- Bake for 45 mins and serve.

SNOW WHITE'S CHICKEN IN WHITE SAUCE

Chicken breasts
4

Mushrooms
9 ounces

Tarragon
1 bunch

Greek-style yogurt
1½ cups

 Salt, pepper

 Oil

 : 4

⏱
Preparation: 5 mins
Cooking time: 20 mins

• In a skillet, sauté the peeled **mushroom** quarters, each cut into four, and the **chicken breasts** cut into pieces with 2 tablespoons of oil.

• Cook for 10 mins. Add the **Greek yogurt** and cook for another 10 mins.

• Season with salt and pepper. Sprinkle with **tarragon** leaves and serve immediately.

WENDY'S CHICKEN

Chicken
1

Broccoli
1 head

Romanesco
1 head

Pesto
2 tablespoons

Bouquets garnis
2, bay leaves and thyme

  **Salt, pepper**

: 5

Preparation: 15 mins
Cooking time: 50 mins

- Preheat the oven to 350°F.
- Brush the **chicken** with **pesto** and place in a large ovenproof dish. Add the **broccoli** and **romanesco**, cut into pieces, 4 cups of water, and the **bouquets garnis**. Season with salt and pepper.
- Cook in the oven for 50 mins and serve.

TIMOTHY AND DUMBO'S DELIGHT

Sirloin steaks
3, thick cut

Snow peas
4 cups

Soy sauce
¼ cup

Ginger
1½-inch piece

Unshelled peanuts
1 cup

 **Salt, pepper**

 Oil

: 4

Preparation: 5 mins
Cooking time: 5 mins

• Blanch the **snow peas** in boiling water for 2 mins.
• Peel and grate the **ginger**. Shell the **peanuts**.
• Brown the **meat** cut into pieces with the **ginger** and 2 tablespoons of oil in a skillet for 2 mins. Add the **snow peas**, **soy sauce**, and **peanuts**, season with salt and pepper, stir, and serve.

MERLIN'S PIE

Basic pie dough 1 quantity, prepared	**Sausage meat** 9 ounces

Ground beef 9 ounces, lean	**Potatoes** 4	**Dried thyme** 1 tablespoon

 Salt, pepper

 : 4

🕐
Preparation: 10 mins
Cooking time: 45 mins

• Preheat the oven to 350°F.
• Peel and dice the **potatoes** and mix with the 2 types of **meat** and **thyme** in a pie plate. Season with salt and pepper and cover with the **pie dough**. Fold over the edges and seal with the tines of a fork.
• Insert two small vents made out of parchment paper and bake for 45 mins. Serve hot.

TIANA'S SWEET POTATO CURRY

Pork shoulder
2½ pounds

Cilantro
1 bunch, chopped

Curry powder
2 tablespoons

Coconut milk
3⅓ cups

Sweet potato
1 large

 Salt, pepper

Oil

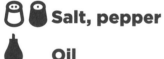 : 4

Preparation: 5 mins
Cooking time: 2 hours

• In a casserole, lightly brown the pieces of **pork** with 2 tablespoons of oil. Add the **coconut milk** and **curry powder**, season, then cover and simmer over low heat for 1 hour and 45 mins.

• Add the diced **sweet potato**, cover, and cook for 15 mins.

• Serve from the dish with **cilantro**.

MERIDA'S TROUT

Rainbow trout
4, whole and gutted

Slivered almonds
¼ cup

Whole hazelnuts
2 tablespoons

Blueberries
2 cups

 Salt, pepper

Oil

 **: 4**

Preparation: 5 mins
Cooking time: 25 mins

- Preheat the oven to 350°F.
- Place the **trout** in a large ovenproof dish and add the crushed **almonds** and **hazelnuts**. Season with salt and pepper, drizzle with 2 tablespoons of oil, and bake for 15 mins .
- Add the **blueberries**, bake for another 10 mins, and serve.

LASAGNA WITH SMOKED SALMON AND SPINACH

Smoked salmon
7 ounces

Light cream
1¼ cups

Spinach
2 (10-ounce) boxes, thawed

Lasagna sheets
10

Olive oil
2 tablespoons

 Pepper

 : 4

⏱

Preparation: 20 mins
Cooking time: 30 mins

- Preheat the oven to 350°F.
- In a large bowl, mix the **spinach**, **cream**, and **smoked salmon** cut into pieces. Season with pepper. Arrange alternate layers of **lasagna sheets** and the spinach mixture in an ovenproof dish.
- Bake for 30 mins and serve drizzled with the **olive oil**.

HUEY, DEWEY, AND LOUIE'S SKEWERS

Salmon steaks
4, 4 ounzes each

Rosemary
8 sprigs

Zucchini
1 large

Soy sauce
2 tablespoons

  Salt, pepper

 Olive oil

 : 4

Preparation: 15 mins
Cooking time: 10 mins

• Preheat the oven to 350°F.

• Cut the **zucchini** into wide strips with a paring knife. Cut the **salmon steaks** into four and wrap in the **zucchini** strips.

• Assemble eight skewers on the **rosemary** sprigs. Season with salt and pepper. Bake the skewers in the oven for 10 mins and serve with the **soy sauce** and a drizzle of olive oil.

PACHA'S CHILI

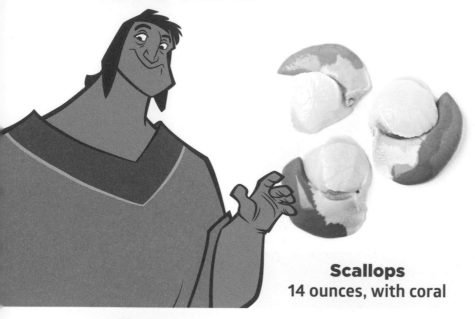

Scallops
14 ounces, with coral

Red kidney beans
3 cups drained, canned

Peeled tomatoes
1¾ cups, canned

Ground cumin
2 tablespoons

 Salt, pepper

 Oil

 **: 4**

🕐

Preparation: 5 mins
Cooking time: 20 mins

• Sauté the **scallops** with 1 tablespoon of oil in a Dutch oven over high heat for 5 mins.

• Add the **peeled tomatoes** with their juice, the **cumin**, and **red kidney beans**. Season with salt and pepper.

• Reduce the heat to low and cook for 15 mins, stirring occasionally, and serve.

152

SALMON FROM HUNDRED-ACRE WOOD

Salmon steaks
4

Granola
2 tablespoons, unsweetened

Unsweetened cranberries
2 tablespoons

Honey
1 tablespoon

Lemons
2

Salt, pepper

: 4

Preparation: 5 mins
Cooking time: 20 mins

• Preheat the oven to 350°F.

• Place the **salmon steaks** in an ovenproof dish and cover with the **granola**. Warm the **honey** with the juice of the **lemons** and pour over the **salmon steaks**. Season with salt and pepper and add the **cranberries**.

• Bake in the oven for 20 mins and serve.

FIGARO'S COD

Tomato
1

Cod fillets
2, about 2¼ pounds

Whole-grain mustard
2 tablespoons

Light cream
1 cup

 Tarragon
1 bunch

 Salt, pepper

 Olive oil

 : 4–5

Preparation: 5 mins
Cooking time: 15 mins

- Preheat the oven to 400°F.
- Cut the **cod fillets** into pieces and arrange in an ovenproof dish with the diced **tomato** and the leaves of half the **tarragon**. Mix the **mustard** with the **cream** and 1 tablespoon of olive oil, then spread over the **fish**. Season with salt and pepper bake for 15 mins.
- Add the remaining **tarragon** leaves and serve.

CHIRASHI SESAME SALMON

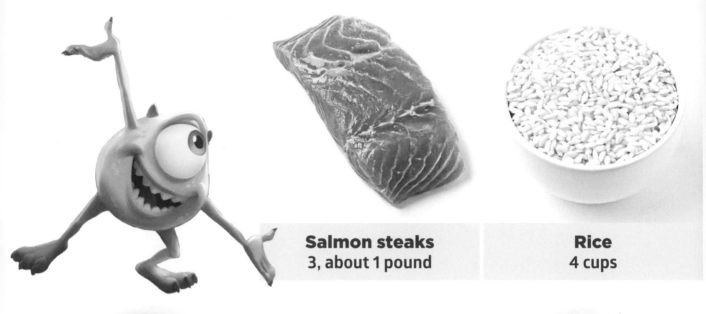

Salmon steaks
3, about 1 pound

Rice
4 cups

Sesame seeds
4 teaspoons

Lemons
2

Sweet soy sauce
¼ cup

 : 4

Preparation: 5 mins
Cooking time: 20 mins
Marination: 5 mins

• Put the **rice** in a large bowl with 8 cups of water. Cover with microwavable plastic wrap and cook for 20 mins in an 800 W microwave.

• Cut the **salmon** into small pieces and mix with the juice of the **lemons**, the **sweet soy sauce**, and **sesame seeds**.

• Marinate for 5 mins and serve with the warm **rice**.

DAVID'S COCONUT AND BASIL FISH

Redfish fillets
4 regular or 8 small

Basil
1 bunch

Tomatoes
4

Coconut milk
1⅔ cups

 **Salt, pepper**

 Olive oil

: 4

**Preparation: 5 mins
Cooking time: 20 mins**

- Preheat the oven to 400°F.
- Mix the **coconut milk** with the **basil** leaves and **tomatoes** cut into pieces. Arrange the **redfish fillets** in an ovenproof dish and pour the mixture over them.
- Season with salt and pepper bake for 20 mins.
- Serve with a drizzle of olive oil.

THE SUSHI CHEF'S SPECIALITY

Glutinous or risotto rice
1⅔ cups

Red tuna
14 ounces

Seasoning
Soy sauce, crystallized ginger, and wasabi

Confectioners' sugar
1 tablespoon

Rice vinegar or apple cider vinegar
⅓ cup

 Salt

 : 4

Preparation: 15 mins
Cooking time: 10 mins
Resting time: 15 mins

• Wash the **rice** thoroughly. Put into a saucepan with 1¼ cups of water, cover, and cook over low heat for 10 mins. Let rest for 15 mins.

• Dissolve the **sugar** in the **vinegar**, pour over the **rice**, season with salt, and stir until completely cold. Form small sausages of **rice**, top with slices of raw **tuna**, and serve with the Japanese **seasoning**.

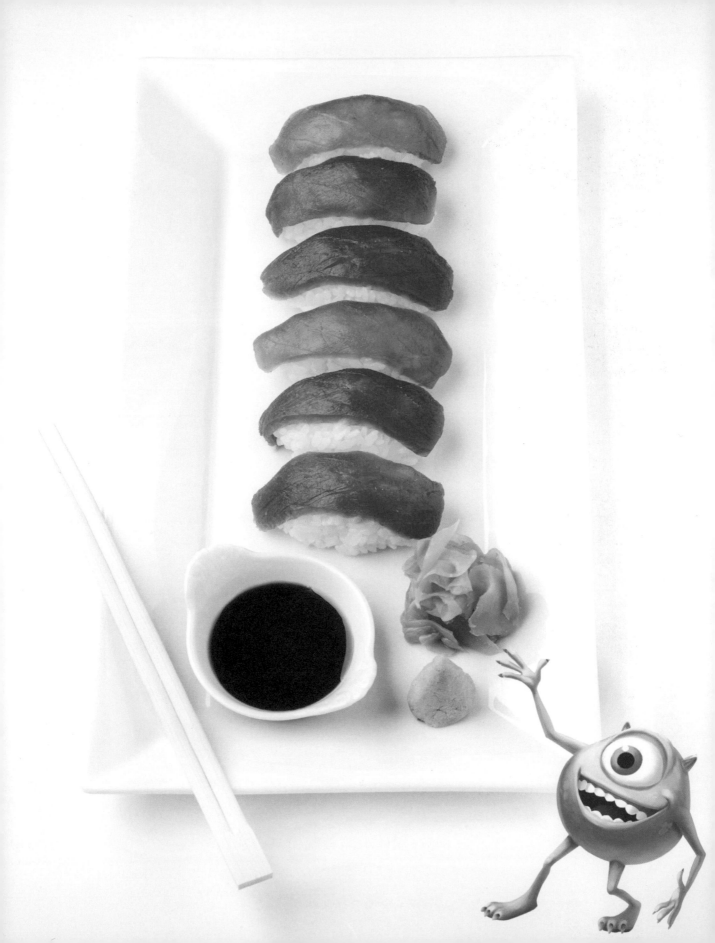

SUPER FITNESS JUICE

Baby spinach
5 cups

Pear
1

Orange
1

Grapefruit
1

Bananas
2

: 4

Preparation: 5 mins

- Cut 1 slice of **orange** for decoration.
- Chop the **baby spinach**, **bananas**, and **pear** into pieces and mix in a blender with the juice of the **orange** and **grapefruit**.
- Pour into glasses. Decorate with the pieces of **orange** and serve immediately.

AFTERNOON SCONES

All-purpose flour
2 cups

Butter
3 tablespoons, softened

Milk
⅔ cup

Brown sugar
1 tablespoon

Baking powder
2½ teaspoons

 : 4

Preparation: 15 mins
Cooking time: 12 mins

- Preheat the oven to 425°F.
- Mix the **flour**, **baking powder**, and **brown sugar** in a large bowl. While kneading with one hand, gradually add the softened **butter** and the **milk**.
- Form balls of dough and arrange on a baking sheet lined with parchment paper.
- Bake for 12 mins and serve.

166

DASH'S CEREAL BARS

Granola	Dried apricots
¾ cup, unsweetened	5

Mixed nuts & dried fruit	Butter	Honey
½ cup	2 tablespoons	¼ cup

 : 4

Preparation: 15 mins
Cooking time: 20 mins

- Preheat the oven to 350°F.
- Melt the **butter** and **honey** in a saucepan and pour over the **granola**, the **apricots** cut into small pieces, and the **mixed nuts & dried fruit**.
- Transfer the mixture to individual loaf pans and bake for 20 mins .
- Let cool, turn out, and enjoy.

MINNIE'S PALMIERS

Puff pastry dough
1 package

Brown sugar
2 tablespoons

  **: 4–5 people**

🕐

Preparation: 5 mins
Cooking time: 25 mins
Freezing time: 30 mins

• Preheat the oven to 350°F.

• Unroll the **puff pastry** with its parchment paper. Sprinkle with the **brown sugar**.

• Roll each side of the **pastry** tightly toward the center to form the palmiers.

• Place in the freezer for 30 mins to firm up. Cut into thin slices and arrange on a baking sheet lined with parchment paper. Bake for 25 mins.

OLAF'S SNOWBALLS

Shredded dry coconut
1¾ cups

Sweetened condensed milk
⅔ cup

Hazelnuts
20

 : 4

Preparation: 15 mins
Refrigeration: 3 hours

• Mix 1½ cups of the **shredded coconut** with the **sweetened condensed milk**. Refrigerate for 3 hours.

• Form 20 balls of the mixture with one hazelnut in the center and coat with the remaining **shredded coconut**.

CHIP 'N' DALE'S BISCOTTI

Hazelnuts
1½ cups

All-purpose flour
2⅓ cups

Baking powder
1¼ teaspoons

Eggs
3

Brown sugar
½ cup packed

 Salt

 : 6–8

Preparation: 10 mins
Cooking time: 20 mins

• Preheat the oven to 350°F.
• Mix together the **brown sugar**, **eggs**, **flour**, **baking powder**, **hazelnuts**, and a pinch of salt.
• Form the dough into small logs about 1¼ inches wide and bake for 20 mins on a baking sheet lined with parchment paper.
• Cut into ⅝-inch slices as soon as they come out of the oven and let cool.

RILEY'S POPCORN TREATS

Apples
4

Greek-style yogurt
1¼ cups

Cinnamon
1 tablespoon

Popping corn
2 tablespoons

Raisins
3 large tablespoons

: 4

Preparation: 5 mins
Cooking time: 11 mins

• Put the **corn** into a large bowl. Cover with pierced microwavable plastic wrap and pop for 3 mins in the microwave.

• Mix the diced **apples** in a bowl with the **raisins** and **cinnamon**. Cover with plastic wrap and cook for 8 mins in the microwave. Arrange the **apples**, **raisins**, **yogurt**, and **popcorn** in glasses and serve.

POOH'S MADELEINES

Butter
1 stick (½ cup)

All-purpose flour
1 cup

Honey
¼ cup

Eggs
2

Baking powder
½ teaspoon

 : 4–5

Preparation: 10 mins
Cooking time: 15 mins

• Preheat the oven to 350°F.
• Melt the **butter** in the microwave. Grease the madeleine pans and set aside the remaining butter.
• Beat the **eggs** with the **honey** for 1 min with an electric mixer. Add the **flour** mixed with the **baking powder** and the melted **butter**.
• Spoon the batter into the pans and bake for 15 mins.

NICK'S FROZEN YOGURT POPS

Yogurt
4 individual containers

Raspberries
1 cup

 : 4

Preparation: 5 mins
Freezing time: 2 hours

• Drain the **yogurts** (reserving the containers) and mix with the crushed **raspberries**.

• Spoon the mixture into the empty containers. Insert a wooden skewer or ice cream stick into each one and freeze for 2 hours.

• Remove the frozen yogurt pops by breaking the containers with the point of a knife and enjoy.

MOWGLI'S BANANA AND MANGO MOUSSE

Bananas
2

Mango
1

Egg whites
2

Lemon
1

: 4

Preparation: 15 mins
Refrigeration: 20 mins

• Peel the **bananas** and set four slices aside. Puree the remainder of the **bananas** with the peeled and diced **mango** and the juice and zest of the **lemon**.

• Beat the **egg whites** until stiff and fold into the fruit puree. Spoon the mousse into cups and top with a slice of **banana**.

• Refrigerate for 20 mins and serve.

THE SEVEN DWARFS' BAKED APPLES

Red apples
8 small

Blackberries
1¾ cups

Honey
2 tablespoons

 : 4

Preparation: 5 mins
Cooking time: 35 mins

- Preheat the oven to 400°F.
- Cut the tops off the **apples** and remove the cores. Bake for 25 mins.
- Fill the cooked apples with the **blackberries**, and **honey**, replace the tops, and bake for another 10 mins.
- Serve hot or cold.

BALOO'S SKEWERS

Mini bananas
4

Kiwis
2

Shredded dry coconut
2 tablespoons

Coconut milk
1 cup

Passion fruits
2

 : 4

Preparation: 10 mins

• Peel the **bananas** and **kiwis** and cut into pieces.
• Assemble four skewers with the pieces of **fruit** and sprinkle with **shredded coconut**.
• Serve with the **coconut milk** mixed with the **passion fruit** flesh.

JASMINE'S ORANGE SALAD

Oranges
5

Blanched pistachios
2 tablespoons

Mint
1 bunch

Orange flower water
¼ cup

Honey
1 tablespoon

 : 4

Preparation: 15 mins

• Remove the peel and pith of four **oranges** with a sharp knife. Slice the **oranges** and arrange in a serving dish.

• Add the crushed **pistachios**, **mint** leaves, the juice of the fifth **orange**, the **orange flower water**, and **honey**.

• Serve chilled.

RAFIKI'S BANANAS

Bananas
2

Maple syrup
¼ cup

Limes
2

: 4

Preparation: 5 mins
Cooking time: 10 mins

• Preheat the oven broiler.
• Cut the **bananas** in half lengthwise, leaving the peels on, and arrange in an ovenproof dish.
• Mix the juice and zest of the **limes** with the **maple syrup** and pour the mixture over the **bananas**.
• Bake for 10 mins and serve hot or cold.

VAIANA'S EXOTIC FRUIT SALAD

Pineapple
1

Passion fruits
2

Mango
1

Star fruit (carambola)
1, sliced

Coconut milk
¼ cup

 : 4

Preparation: 10 mins

• Cut the **pineapple** in half, scoop out the flesh, and cut into small pieces. Peel and dice the **mango**. Scoop out the flesh of the **passion fruits** and mix with the **coconut milk**.

• Mix all the ingredients in the **pineapple** shells, add the **star fruit**, and serve chilled.

HARRIS, HUBERT, AND HAMISH'S DESSERT

Berries
3½ cups

Almond meal
1¼ cups

Butter
1¾ sticks (⅞ cup), softened

Brown sugar
½ cup packed

All-purpose flour
1 cup

 Confectioners' sugar

 : 8

🕐
Preparation: 10 mins
Cooking time: 30 mins

- Preheat the oven to 400°F.
- Mix the **flour**, **butter**, **brown sugar**, and **almond meal** to a smooth dough. Add the **berries** and mix.
- Transfer the dough to a rectangular tart pan lined with parchment paper. Press down and bake for 30 mins.
- Let cool and dust with **confectioners' sugar**.

SNOW WHITE'S PLUM TART

Puff pastry dough
1 sheet

Plums
8

Slivered almonds
1¼ cups

 : 4

Preparation: 10 mins
Cooking time: 30 mins

- Preheat the oven to 400°F.
- Pit the **plums** and cut into pieces.
- Unroll the **puff pastry** on to parchment paper and press into a tart pan. Spread with the **plums** and 1 cup of the **almonds**. Fold over the edges. Sprinkle with the remaining **almonds**.
- Bake for 30 mins and serve.

THE MAD HATTER'S PIE

Basic pie dough
1 quantity prepared

Rhubarb
8 stalks

Strawberries
1⅔ cups hulled

Brown sugar
2 tablespoons

 : 4

Preparation: 5 mins
Cooking time: 25 mins

- Preheat the oven to 350°F.
- In a saucepan, cook the trimmed **rhubarb** and **strawberries** cut into pieces with the **brown sugar** over low heat for 10 mins.
- Spoon the fruit into individual dishes, top with strips of **pie dough**, and bake for 15 mins.
- Serve warm or cold.

AURORA'S BERRY CRISP

All-purpose flour
¾ cup

Butter
1 stick (½ cup), softened

Brown sugar
½ cup packed

Mixed berries
4 cups, fresh or frozen

 : 4

Preparation: 5 mins
Cooking time: 30 mins

- Preheat the oven to 350°F.
- With your fingertips, mix the **butter**, **flour**, and **brown sugar** to a crumb dough.
- Cover the bottom of an ovenproof dish with 3 cups of the **berries**. Add the crumb dough and then the remaining **berries**. Bake for 30 mins and serve.

MOTHER RABBIT'S BREAD PUDDING

Stale bread
8 slices

Eggs
4

Honey
6 tablespoons

Milk
2 cups

Raisins
½ cup

 Butter
(for greasing)

 : 6

🕐

Preparation: 5 mins
Waiting time: 15 mins
Cooking time: 30 mins

- Preheat the oven to 350°F.
- Beat the **eggs**, then add the **milk** and 5 tablespoons of the **honey**. Add the **stale bread** torn into small pieces and the **raisins**. Let soak for 15 mins.
- Transfer to a greased loaf pan and bake for 30 mins. Turn out and serve in thick slices with the remaining **honey**.

RUSSELL'S CRUNCHY MOUSSE

Semisweet chocolate
7 ounces

Eggs
3

Granola
3 tablespoons (unsweetened)

Honey
2 tablespoons

 : 6

Preparation: 15 mins
Refrigeration: 2 hours
Cooking time: 10 mins

• Melt the **chocolate** and mix with the **egg yolks**. Beat the **whites** until stiff and fold into the melted **chocolate**. Spoon into ramekins and refrigerate to set for 2 hours.

• Preheat the oven to 350°F. Bake the **granola** mixed with the **honey** for 10 mins on a baking sheet lined with parchment paper. Let cool, crush, and sprinkle it over the mousses.

EDGAR'S VANILLA CREAM

Vanilla beans
3

Eggs
8

Milk
3 cups

Brown sugar
⅔ cup packed

 : 6

Preparation: 5 mins
Cooking time: 40 mins
Refrigeration: 3 hours

• Preheat the oven to 325°F.

• Scrape out the contents of the **vanilla beans**. Beat the **eggs** with the **brown sugar**, add the **milk**, **vanilla** seeds, and the **beans** cut into pieces. Mix, transfer to a dish, place in a baking pan filled partway with water, and bake for 40 mins.

• Refrigerate for 3 hours and serve.

CONTENTS

CONTENTS

INDEX OF RECIPES BY INGREDIENT

INDEX

INDEX

INDEX

NOTES

NOTES

© 2018 Disney Enterprises, Inc. All rights reserved.
Pixar properties © Disney/Pixar
The 101 Dalmatians, after the book by Dodie Smith, published by The Viking Press.
The film *The Princess and the Frog* Copyright © 2009 Disney, story partly inspired by the book *The Frog Princess* by E. D. Baker Copyright © 2003, published by Bloomsbury Publishing, Inc.
Winnie the Pooh, after the original book *Winnie the Pooh* by A. A. Milne, illustrated by E. H. Shepard.
The Aristocats is based on the book by Thomas Rowe.
The Rescuers and *The Rescuers Down Under* feature characters from the Disney film suggested by the books by Margery Sharp, *The Rescuers and Miss Bianca*, published by Little, Brown and Company.
Mr. Potato Head® is a registered trademark of Hasbro, Inc. Used with permission. © Hasbro, Inc. All rights reserved.
© 2018, Hachette Livre (Hachette Pratique)
English translation copyright © Octopus Publishing Group 2018

An Hachette UK Company
www.hachette.co.uk

First published in Great Britain in 2018 by Ilex,
a division of Octopus Publishing Group Ltd
Carmelite House
50 Victoria Embankment
London EC4Y 0DZ
www.octopusbooks.co.uk

Originally published in France in 2018 by Hachette Livre (Hachette Pratique)
www.hachette-pratique.com

Title of the original edition: Simplissime : La cuisine en famille la + facile du monde avec Disney
Interior layout: Marie-Paule Jaulme et SKGD-création

Distributed in the US by
Hachette Book Group
1290 Avenue of the Americas
4th and 5th Floors
New York, NY 10104

Distributed in Canada by
Canadian Manda Group
664 Annette St.
Toronto, Ontario, Canada M6S 2C8

All rights reserved. No part of this work may be reproduced or utilised in any form or by any means, electronic or mechanical, including photocopying, recording or by any information storage and retrieval system, without the prior written permission of the publisher.

Ilex
Licensing Director: Roly Allen
Publishing Assistant: Stephanie Hetherington
Managing Editor: Rachel Silverlight

Translation from French: Rae Walter in association with First Edition Translation Ltd, Cambridge, UK.

ISBN 978-1-781-57667-0

A CIP catalogue record for this book is available from the British Library.

Printed and bound in China

10 9 8 7 6 5 4 3 2 1